# Awareness Games

## *Playing with Your Mind to Create Joy*

Brian Tom O'Connor

Published by Slippery Mind

ISBN-13: 978-0692628638

ISBN-10: 0692628630


www.playawarenessgames.com

*For my parents, Dan (who lives in our memory) and Lenka*
*and the rest of their Jolly O'Connor Kids:*
*Kevin, Darren, Glynnis, and Sean*
*(they laugh, they sing, they laugh ha ha they sing tra la).*
*And to Josh, an honorary Jolly O'Connor Kid*

# *Contents*

# Awareness Games

An infinite well of happiness and joy lies within each of us, and people from all cultures have been sending reports from there for thousands of years. I've stumbled upon it within me, so let's see if you can find it too. I bet we all can experience it if we know where to look. And where not to look.

It doesn't appear in the outside world. It doesn't appear in thoughts or concepts. It doesn't appear in anything you can give a name to—which makes it kind of tough to describe in words.

But anyone can experience it with a little shift in the direction of attention. You can sense it by shifting your point of view from the content of awareness to awareness itself. Of course, this is easier said than done, so we have to approach if from whatever angle works for us. Sometimes we have to approach it sideways instead of directly. Sometimes the effort we exert to try to see it is the very thing that obscures it.

Each of us needs to find what "clicks" for us, because this well of love and joy is a little bit tricky to find. In fact, we have to stumble around until we accidentally fall into it. There are no specific maps. That's where games come in—because when we're playing a game we're letting go of the idea that only certain things work and certain other things don't work. We're experimenting—we're playing—we're stumbling—we're hoping to accidentally fall into this well because we're playing around it.

And when we stumble into it we realize that it's not something separate from us—it *is* us. We can identify with this pure ground of being, and when we do, we can discover that love and joy pervade everything—even pain. It's not that pain miraculously disappears, but that we come to see pain as *made of* love, and this seeing transforms our experience of pain.

Another reason this limitless spring of happiness and love is tricky to find is because it's invisible to the part of the mind that we use most of the time every day. It's invisible to the part of the mind that looks for differences between things, but it's visible to the part of the mind that allows all opposites to exist—the part of the mind that doesn't filter or categorize. It can be sensed by looking inside and becoming aware of awareness itself—becoming aware of pure background, pure subjectivity.

The mind is the organ of separation. Its job is to scan the environment and distinguish between the good stuff and the bad stuff—the stuff that will help us survive and the stuff that's dangerous. But the mind is a tool—it's not us. It's something we use—it's something we're aware of—it looks at objects. In fact, thought itself is an object. What's aware of thought? What is thought appearing to? That's pure subjectivity.

This is nothing new. People have been stumbling upon it for thousands of years and describing the experience in almost as many ways as there are people describing it. But when people hear about it, a funny thing happens. The mind takes it on as its job—a problem to solve or figure out. But the mind is a thirsty fish, forever looking for water by analyzing its surroundings to figure out what's water and what's not water, not realizing it's *all* water. The mind can't see pure awareness because the mind is *in* pure awareness, like a fish is in water.

Nonetheless, pure awareness can be known, but only when the mind takes a rest, or is distracted, or gives up. That's why we play games with it. We play with our mind by setting up various little goals that short-circuit the usual mind business of figuring things out.

These are not Olympic Games or board games with winners and losers. These are not the games of game theorists (as fascinating as their theories are) or of competitive players (as enjoyable as their games can be). They are fun ways to sidestep all the ways the mind sorts the outside world, and instead, points it within to look for its own source. Playing these games is not like playing a video game with points to win and things to destroy and goals to reach. It's more like playing with toys. The toys are your mind, your awareness, your innermost self. (I was tempted to call this book *Playing With Your Self*, but I came to my senses.)

All of these Awareness Games have one purpose: to turn the mind around from outer focus to inner focus, and through inner focus to find that obscure little secret passageway to expanded focus. The delightful surprise is that the obscure little secret passageway was hiding in plain sight all along.

### Why Games?

Why games? Why not practices, techniques, meditations, questions, koans, disciplines, instructions?

Because finding the well of joy within is not something with correct answers, set rules, reproducible steps. Everyone is different, so everyone must experiment (that is, play around) and stumble upon what works for each person. The best way to do this is with an attitude of lightness, playfulness, ease, innocent curiosity.

Because you don't have to believe anything to play a game. If I try to teach you something, your mind runs it through the truth-checker. Is it true? Is it not true? Is it a crock? With a game, it doesn't matter. The only thing that matters is what you find out for yourself while you're playing around. You don't have to believe in any metaphysical, theological, philosophical, religious, spiritual, or even scientific concept. You just have to try it.

Because correctness and seriousness hinder the search. In some senses, even searching hinders the search! How can you search for something that is already here—that you already have? And yet just sitting around watching TV may not do the trick either.

Also because I like to have fun.

So play with your awareness like a toy—bounce it, squeeze it, smell it, shake it, become immersed in it. You may discover you *are* it. But don't take my word for it—play with it yourself.

## *Why Me?*

Who am I to be writing about awareness? I don't claim to be an enlightened person. I'm just a guy who has experienced a lot of fear, anxiety, inhibition, and depression, and who was determined to find an alternative to suffering.

I'd had enough glimpses of natural happiness to know what I was looking for. Even though they were fleeting and I couldn't bring them about at will, I knew from remembering the taste what to be on the lookout for. Plus, I've gotten guidance along the way from some expert teachers—both in person and through writings and recordings.

Like most people, I tried a lot of things, some helpful, some not, and a pattern began to emerge among the teachers and writers I kept coming back to. I waded through a lot of dead ends, false starts, and pure wishful thinking, but the material that rang true for me all had certain elements in common: It's not out there, it's inside you. It's not about controlling experience, it's about experience itself. It's about a shift in identity from the content of awareness to awareness itself. It's not about what you're looking at, but about what's looking.

These themes kept cropping up over and over again in reports from all cultures and all ages—that is, if the reports had a genuine flavor of the truth of first-hand experience.

But I also realized that I couldn't simply think my way there, or believe what others believe, or even follow the steps that others prescribe. I could only experiment with myself and find my own way. I'm still in the process of doing that, and I invite you to join me.

Plus, just the act of writing down the games brings that "happy for no reason" feeling that the games are designed to achieve. Same with telling people about the games (if they're interested). So I decided, why wait for enlightenment? Play the games, write them down, and share them with others.

So try the games and make up your own. Experiment. See what works for you. It's all about *your* direct experience.

### Using Questions

One of the basic elements of all the games is the question. In fact, you might notice that practically all of the games are comprised of questions. So why call them games? Why not just call them Awareness Questions? Good question. It's because coming up with an answer is not the goal of these questions. The questions trigger the looking inward, and the looking inward is something that's made easier by a playful, curious, experimental attitude. Asking *is* the game. The act of asking is the game of "aware-ing."

Many of the questions are "what if?" questions. "What if" does not ask you to believe "this is." "What if" only asks you to entertain for a few moments a possibility you may not have entertained before. If it goes against all of your mind's ideas, beliefs, and principles, then remember it's only a temporary "what if." You can return to the way you believe things are in a little bit. Or not—who knows? It's just a game.

# *The Basic Awareness Questions*

All the games are variations on three basic questions. Try them out on yourself, then play some of the games and come back to these questions. Keep coming back to them whenever you think of it. In fact, if you forget how to play any of the games, or lose this book, or give it away, or throw it away, or sell it on eBay, you can simply remember to remember to ask yourself these three questions:

1. What is *in* awareness?

2. What *is* awareness?

3. What is *aware?*

Let's take them one by one.

*1. What is in awareness?* This simply means, what am I aware of? What are the contents of awareness? What sights, sounds, smells, sensations, objects, thoughts, emotions swim into my field of awareness at any given moment? Take an inventory of awareness: "Let's see, there's the sounds outside and in the room... there's the breeze on my face... there's the feeling of my body against my clothes and against the chair. There's a taste inside my mouth... There are colors and shapes and light coming in through my eyes—or the darkness behind my eyelids if they're closed... There are thoughts running through my head. There are emotions playing through my mind and body..."

*2. What is awareness?* Ok, I know what I'm aware *of,* but what actually *is* this thing called awareness? Look at it. Try to find it. Become aware of it—awareness becoming aware of awareness.

*3. What is aware?* Who or what is it appearing to? Who or what is doing the "aware-ing"? Is it my body? But I'm aware of my body, aren't I? So what's aware of *it*? Is it my thoughts? But I'm aware of my thoughts, aren't I? So what's aware of *them*? This is the shift, the "backwards step," the little turn-around from what is noticed to what is noticing.

If your answer to the question "What is aware?" turns out to be "I am," then ask "Who am I?" Or better, "What am I?" Then continue as above, with the further questions, "Am I my name? — "Who has a name?" "Am I my body? — Who has a body?" "Am I my thoughts? — Who has thoughts?"

The idea is not to come up with an answer. The idea is to ask a question that triggers a shift in perspective from foreground to background. Be the background. Let the foreground be whatever it wants to be.

What is aware? Awareness is aware. Be awareness.

# *What is Awareness?*

Awareness is a tricky concept for a lot of people at first. When you look for awareness, you might not know what you're looking for. So let's start with a definition of what awareness is, and then move to what awareness is not.

### *What is awareness?*

Awareness is what's noticing your current experience.

Awareness is what everything you can possibly notice appears in.

Awareness is the noticing of everything that can be noticed, including the noticing itself.

Awareness is what doesn't change when everything else in your experience changes.

Awareness is the background of your experience.

Awareness is the background to everything you notice.

Awareness is what's looking.

Awareness is what's hearing.

Awareness is what thought appears to.

Awareness is what sensations appear to.

Awareness is what emotions appear to.

Awareness is what dreams appear in.

Awareness is what has never changed since you were a little child.

Awareness is where you go when you ask, "Am I aware?"

Awareness is you.

### *Is awareness a thing?*

Not really. Like an empty space it has no features of its own. Like a blank page it has nothing written on it yet. Like a blank canvas it has nothing painted on it yet. Like a blank tape it has nothing recorded on it yet.

But unlike those examples, it keeps its quality of emptiness when something appears in its space; it keeps its quality of blankness when something is written on it. It keeps its quality of silence when sound is recorded on it.

But even that's not it. It's not an "it." It shouldn't even really be a noun. It's more like a verb... more like "aware-ing."

### What is awareness NOT?

It's not a special state you have to get to. It's already happening even if you don't notice.

It's not a mystical or special experience. It's just garden-variety everyday awareness. The simple noticing of experience.

It's not something you have to learn to do. It's already doing itself. You simply notice it.

It's not a concept.

### What do you mean by the content of awareness, as opposed to awareness itself?

Content:

- objects you see
- objects you touch
- sounds you hear
- sensations you feel
- thoughts in your head
- images in your head
- emotions you feel
- concepts you think of
- ideas you have
- other people
- your body
- anything you can think of
- anything you can notice
- anything you can or see, hear, taste, smell, or touch.

Awareness itself:

- what all of the above appears to.

# *Rules That Apply to All the Games*

- Relax.

- Get curious. Assume you don't know until you look.

- If you get distracted, just gently focus back. No need to kick yourself—it happens all the time to everybody.

- Play as often as you can.

- If you enjoy long sessions of play, fine. If you don't like to play for long stretches at a time, go for short periods several times a day.

- Use the least amount of effort possible.

- It's not about control, except for the slightest shift in attention—a shift of focus while letting everything be as it is.

### *The Main Goals of All the Games*

All the games have the same goals. It's only the way to play that changes from game to game. So the key goals of all the games are:

- a shift in focus from object to subject, from what's noticed to what's noticing

- letting go of control

- shifting from verbal or conceptual thought to direct experience

- effortless awareness—clear and mirror-like.

A mirror doesn't choose what to reflect; doesn't require any effort to reflect; doesn't distort or interpret what it reflects; doesn't control or affect what it reflects; and isn't affected by what it reflects. Awareness is like that. Awareness Games are ways to *be* the mirror to your experience.

### How Do I Know I'm Playing It Right?

- Is it fun?

- Is there something inside that eases?  A relaxation of tension, a letting go of clutching?

- Do you crack a smile without trying to?

- Do you get a feeling of expansion or spaciousness?

- Do you start to get a slight inkling that maybe the world is in you instead of you being in the world?

- Do you start to get the feeling that what you're looking for is already here, inside you?  Not even inside you, but actually you?

These are all clues that you're on the right track—even if only one of these is happening. (The one about cracking a smile was a major tip-off for me.)

Try some games, and if you feel you're not quite getting the hang of it, take a look at the "Tips and Traps" chapter after the games. Then try again, or try some different games. All you really need is one that clicks for you.

Let's play.

# *THE GAMES*

## *Expanding and Contracting Awareness*

- Contract your awareness down to one thing: a toe; a thought.

- Expand to include more and more of what you are aware of.

- Play with expanding and contracting—how small can you contract to? How large can you expand to? How fast or slow can you expand and contract? Go back and forth. Fiddle with it. Play with it.

We usually think of expanded awareness as some sort of vague mystical new age thing, but I'm talking about literally expanding and contracting. Contract down to the thought stream and then expand to include all the input from all the senses. Include the thought stream, but notice how it shrinks in relation to everything else that you are aware of. When awareness is expanded as much as possible, include awareness itself.

This is a great game to start with, because it's not aiming for a particular result. Its purpose is to give you a feel for playing with your own awareness, like you would with a toy. Experiment.

## The (Your) Name Game

- Imagine your parents haven't given you a name yet. Who are you?

- Then imagine they give you a name and didn't tell you what it is. What does that have to do with you? Are you the same with or without the name?

- What if I had no name?

This is a fun way to start to separate awareness from concepts. After all, a name is just a concept—a tag, a handle. It's not who you are. Shakespeare said it best (as he often did):

> Thou art thyself, though not a Montague.
> What's Montague? It is nor hand nor foot,
> Nor arm nor face, nor any other part
> Belonging to a man. O be some other name!
> What's in a name? That which we call a rose
> By any other word would smell as sweet;
> So Romeo would, were he not Romeo call'd,
> Retain that dear perfection which he owes
> Without that title. Romeo, doff thy name,
> And for thy name, which is no part of thee,
> Take all myself.
>
> Romeo and Juliet (Act 2, Scene 2)

Check it out for thyself and see if thy name is no part of thee.

## *Looking Out Through Other People's Eyes*

- Walk around the streets of your city or town.

- Start by imagining yourself looking outwards from behind your eyes. Get a sense of what it's like to be "me looking at them."

- Then randomly select a person and imagine looking out through his or her eyes. Imagine what it's like to be that person's mind looking out at the world.

- Imagine—just for now if you don't believe it to be true—that what's looking out their eyes is identical to what's looking out your eyes.

- Imagine—just for now if you don't believe it to be true—that what's looking out their eyes is not only identical but exactly the same thing as what's looking out your eyes.

## *Wandering Awareness*

*Let it wander, watch it wander*

Often when we play these games we fall into the trap of trying too hard to limit our awareness to what we'd like to be aware of at the moment. But awareness has a tendency to flit about from thing to thing. Sometimes it's a sound, sometimes it's a thought; sometimes it's a feeling in your body.

- So let awareness wander.
- And simply watch it wander without attempting to "drive" awareness.

Again, the idea is to use the least amount of effort possible to remain aware of what's in awareness, without controlling awareness in any way.

## *Could I Not Be Aware?*

- Play with this: Is it possible to not be aware? To not be aware of anything?

- Do you need to actively choose to be aware?

- Are you ever *not* aware?

The idea of this game is to see if you have to *do* awareness, or if it does itself.

## *Breath Awareness*

*A pair of games to play while you're breathing*

### *Catch Yourself Breathing*

This is another one of those games where you win if you lose. You also win if you win.

- Think of something other than your breathing for a bit.

- Then surprise yourself, and try to notice your breathing *without* changing or altering your breathing in any way.

If you are breathing fast, don't try to breathe more slowly. If your breathing is shallow, don't try to breathe more deeply. The amazing thing is—if you're like me—as soon as you notice your breathing, it changes somehow, sometimes a lot, sometimes in very subtle ways.

So it's fun to try to catch yourself when you're not expecting to be noticing your breath and see if you can notice it without changing it.

As I mentioned before, do this for fun, but don't be surprised if you don't succeed. You succeed if you fail, and you succeed if you succeed, because a) noticing your breath is beneficial, and b) noticing your breath tends to relax, slow down, and deepen your breath, which are good things too.

### *Noticing Noticing Breathing*

Once you've tried "Catch Yourself Breathing" for a while, try this one.

- Notice what's noticing your breathing.

You can also think of this as awareness *around* your breathing.

## *The Passenger*

*Riding Your Experience*

What if, instead of driving your experience, you're in the passenger seat, and you're riding your experience. Someone else is driving. (It doesn't matter who, but since this is your game and your imagination, it can be anything from God, to the entire universe, to an imaginary bus driver, to that mysterious "nothing" that drives everything.)

- Imagine you are riding around inside the vehicle of yourself looking out at the world through the windows of your eyes.

- Imagine you are not the driver of your experience, but the passenger.

- Imagine all your sensations are the terrain you're driving over (it's an all-terrain vehicle), and whatever you pass over or by is ok— you're just riding.

- Imagine all your thoughts, and emotions are the terrain as well (it really is an all-terrain vehicle).

## *Born Yesterday*

*Also known as "The Just Born Identity"*

- Imagine you were just born a little while ago.

- Imagine you haven't learned of the words or concepts or fears or ideas about yourself and the world that you have accumulated up to now.

*Then play the next game...*

## *No Memory / No Imagination*

*What do you know without memory or imagination?*

- Ask yourself: If I don't go to memory, what do I know?
- Ask yourself: If I don't go to imagination, what do I know?

This game is about now—no past (memory), no future (imagination).

Don't get me wrong. You don't have to believe memory is bad or imagination is wrong. In fact, these are wonderfully useful tools of human creativity. But they are abstract tools. They're tools of the mind. They don't really have any physical substance or reality outside of the ideas in the mind.

Memory is not direct experience. Imagination is not direct experience.

You may ask, hey, don't you use imagination in these Awareness Games? Yes, but even here it's only a tool—a tool to trigger a direct experience. Once the tool does its job, you can toss it or lay it aside until you need it again.

## No Intention

*What if you had no intention whatsoever?*

One of my first tastes of this silly blissful feeling came when I heard a quote from the Indian teacher, HWL Poonja, also known as Papaji. Papaji said, "Don't have any intention."

So I asked myself, "What would it be like if I had no intention?" Something inside let go, and I just started to laugh. Part of the laughter was the absurdity of it all. "How can I have no intention? Isn't the intention of having no intention an intention?"

But the bigger part of the laughter is the joy of relief that arises when you're not trying to do anything, to make anything happen, or to control your experience in any way. Something deep inside relaxes, allowing you to simply enjoy what's happening right now.

- So see how long you can go without having any intention whatsoever. Except for this one.

## *Twin Games: Nothing / Everything*

*Imagining Nothing*

- Try to picture this: What if there was nothing?

*Imagining Only One Thing*

- Try to picture this: What if there was only one thing?

The first of these twin games was the first awareness-type game I played as a little kid, although I didn't think of it as such at the time. I remember lying in bed and thinking, "What if there was nothing?" It was difficult to imagine, but I kept trying. After all, if there was nothing, there would be no me to notice that there was nothing, so how can it even be imagined? As I was trying to imagine it, all of a sudden this weird but also weirdly pleasant feeling came over me. An enjoyably scary feeling that was so abstract I couldn't even describe it to myself in words. But I liked it and was fascinated by it. So I made a game of it. Whenever I found myself in bed but not sleepy, I would see if I could get that strange but fun feeling back by thinking, "What if there was nothing?"

The second game is the opposite—or the complement—of the first. What if everything was really only one thing taking on different forms and shapes? Like all the characters and places and objects in a movie are all part of one projected picture. What if, when I move my hand from left to right through the air, it was just the air taking on the shape of a hand, first on the left, and then on the right. I know this may not make sense physics-wise. We know that your hand pushes the air and causes a disturbance. But the object of the game is not to make sense physics-wise—it's to cause a little shift in your awareness.

What if everything was simply one big complex wave taking on the appearance of separate objects? Imagine all of reality was simply matter waving. Ok, this is starting to get conceptual, and the idea here is to experience awareness, not to figure out what reality is conceptually. So try this: Imagine that everything in your awareness, including your body, is all part of the same TV picture. When you move about, the screen isn't physically moving, it's just changing color and brightness in the spot where you were and in the spot where you're moving to.

Don't think too much, or attempt to figure out whether it's actually true or not, just try to imagine it and play with it.

## *Outside In*

*Experiencing the outer world inside*

For everything outside of you that you experience, there is a representation of it inside. That's one way to look at it. Another way to look at it is that all of experience happens inside you. You don't have to believe it's true in order to play with it—just play with it and see what it's like.

The next two games are examples of this with sounds and sights:

### Outside and Inside Sounds

- Listen to the sounds of your environment. Whatever sounds are occurring.
- At first you'll probably perceive them as occurring outside of yourself. But where are you experiencing the sounds?
- What if the sounds are happening inside of you?

### Outside and Inside Sights

- Look at your environment and notice the sights. Whatever sights are occurring.
- At first you'll probably see them as occurring outside of yourself. But where are you experiencing the sights?
- What if the sights are happening inside of you?

Or you can try it with music:

### Feeling Music on the Inside

- Listen to music and notice the inner feeling of music.

Since sounds are vibrations, this is not so far-fetched. You can actually feel sounds sometimes. You can feel music inside of you.

This is a tricky one, though, because music is so attractive and fascinating that it can lure you into thinking about it and getting lost in thought. If that happens, gently remind yourself to feel the music as if it's playing inside of you.

Or you can try it with everything:

### Experience Everything on the Inside

- Imagine everything that's happening is happening inside of you.

- Start with just everything within your vision or earshot...

- ...and then include everything that's happening that you know about...

- ...and then include everything in the world that's happening everywhere.

## *Inside Out*

*Mind Projection*

Normally we think of images and sounds coming from the outside world, through our eyes and ears, and into our brains. This game plays with the opposite.

- Imagine that you're a projector, like a 3-D movie projector, throwing images and sounds out into the world, literally creating it.

- So as you walk around, or just sit and look around, the things and people you see are being created in your mind and projected onto a giant wrap-around 3-D movie screen, with surround sound.

Again, you don't have to believe that this is the way the universe actually works in order to benefit from playing this game. You just have to pretend it works that way for the duration of the game.

## *Zoom In and Zoom Out*

*Narrow and Wide Focus*

This is similar to the "Expanding and Contracting Awareness" game, but from a slightly different angle.

When we get lost in thought, or when we are tackling a specific problem, our focus narrows down to include only the subject at hand and to exclude extraneous awareness.

So try zooming in and zooming out:

- Narrow down to one thing, like wiggling your fingers or reading a sentence, or drawing a stick figure.

- Then zoom out to include everything that is entering into your five senses right now. Zoom out to also include everything you're thinking and feeling right now.

- Then zoom back in again to the topic or task.

- Then zoom out again.

Play with zooming in and out, until you find that at any given moment you can zoom out to include everything at the drop of a hat. Including the hat.

## *Clutch Gobbler*

- Imagine a little Pac-Man-like creature that searches for any tension or clutching inside and eats it up, leaving relaxation in its wake.

This is a fun way to relax. It's also a great way to deal with anxiety.

Every thought that things aren't the way you want them to be causes an internal clutching, or tightening. Every fear or anxiety or bad memory or frustration or angry feeling has a corresponding internal clutching.

So let go of clutching whenever you can. The Clutch Gobbler is a fun way to do it.

Or if you're a manual transmission enthusiast, just try this simple game:

### *Letting Out the Clutch*

- Ask yourself: Am I clutching?
- Where am I clutching?
- Ease out the clutch.

## *Emotion Painting*

*Don't try to change your feeling—paint your feeling*

- Paint a picture of an emotion by describing it physically.

- Where am I feeling it? In what part of my body?

- What does it look like? What shape is it?

- What texture?

- What color is it?

There are (at least) two ways to play this one:  In the first way, you paint a picture in your mind of the emotion. In the second way, you paint *with* the emotion. You imagine the emotion is actually doing the painting—slapping the paint on with huge strokes of a big wide brush, or dotting the paint on with a fine pointy brush, or layering it on in thick gobs of impasto, or delicately stroking in a fine wash of watercolor, or pouring and splattering it on straight from the can with a stick. Whatever seems true to the emotion as you're feeling it right now.

## *Without Thought*

*Game and Variations*

### Wordlessness

*Abstract vs. Verbal Thought*

Do you hear that voice in your head that seems to be continually talking? Is that the only thing that's going on in your head? Sometimes it seems that way, but I bet there's a lot more going on in there. It's just that sometimes that voice distracts you from everything else. That voice is verbal thought.

But it's not the only kind. There are also visual images, sounds and perceptions.

The trick is not to avoid verbal thought, but just to notice how much is going on inside that's not verbal—sometimes called *wordlessness*. When you get some practice at telling the difference, it's easier to ignore the incessant chatter by simply focusing on what else is going on.

Let non-verbal awareness expand—and crowd out verbal thought—until it fills up your whole self.

Try this:

- How long can I go without words going through my mind?

If you fail pretty quickly (join the club), laugh it off and try again. See how long you can stay in Wordlessness.

(A nod to Martha Beck for the word "wordlessness.")

*And now for the variations:*

### Word Erasing

- Imagine the world as you look at it with all the written words erased from all the signs, all the books, all the advertising.

- Imagine all written words have disappeared from the world.
- If you're having fun with this, imagine all talking has disappeared from the world.
- Imagine all words have been erased from your thoughts. Only non-verbal thoughts remain.

*Note: Some people feel there are no thoughts that are not verbal. In other words, they define thought as the words in their heads. That's fine. If you define thought that way, then, instead of verbal thoughts vs. non-verbal thoughts, think of it as thoughts vs. images, or thoughts vs. experiences.*

## No Thoughts, No Past

- Try to imagine the past without thought. Does the past exist without thought?

For this one, I'm referring to both verbal and non-verbal thoughts. So no words running through your mind, and no movies—not even silent movies—running through your mind. What happens to the past then?

## Without Story

Everybody has a story about themselves. We've all been collecting our own and adding to it and rewriting it and polishing it and retelling it our whole verbal lives.

- What if you completely forgot your story?
- Would you be the same person?

(A nod to Byron Katie, who wrote a whole book about this one, *Who Would You Be Without Your Story?*)

## *I Am dot dot dot*

This one's kind of the opposite of Word Erasing, above. This game involves visualizing words as they're being written.

- Visualize the words "I am..."

- Think of an end to the sentence, and visualize it being written

- Erase it. Erase the end of the sentence you added, leaving only "I am..."

- Repeat as many times as you like.

- Or if you're visualizing typing on a computer screen, visualize back-spacing the added part, back to the "I am..."

Examples:

"I am... (insert your name here)" Erase back to the dots

"I am a... (insert gender description of choice here)." Erase back to the dots

"I am a... (insert occupation of choice here)." Erase back to the dots

"I am... (insert self-description of choice here)." Erase back to the dots

## *The I Slide*

*The source of I—Where does that arise from?*

- Think the thought "I."

- Imagine it's a slide that starts in the front of your brain, and goes down, back, within yourself, and ends (or begins) who knows where.

- Slide down it!

Maybe you'll land in the source of "I."  Or in the eye of Source.

# Include, Include, Include

*The game for tough emotions*

Sometimes painful emotions wash over you and demand your attention like a siren or an alarm clock that won't go off. They pull your focus in, narrowing it down, as if to say "Deal with me! Don't think of anything else! Fix this!"

When this happens, it's sometimes difficult to shift your focus to awareness of the emotions. Every time you try to shift to awareness, thoughts about the emotional situation pull you back, as if you're trying to pry open a spring loaded trap, and it keeps snapping shut.

When this happens try this:

- Just for a few seconds, don't try to fix it or make it go away.

- Imagine the emotion is showing up in awareness. In other words, there's the emotion, and there's awareness of the emotion.

- Include more:
  What else is in awareness other than this nasty unwanted feeling? Sounds? Sights? Sensations? Other feelings? Thoughts?

- Include even more.

- Include, include, include. Expand awareness until it includes every possible thing.

The idea is to put that emotion in perspective. Like a jealous lover, it wants to be the only object of your attention. But as insistent as it seems, it really isn't the only thing that's going on right now, although it wants you to believe it is. So don't fight it, just include everything else along with it. The more the merrier.

## *Abstract Art*

If you hate abstract art, feel free to skip this one. If you love it, this might be fun for you.

- Look at some abstract art, like Jackson Pollack, Wassily Kandinsky, Joan Mitchell, Mark Tobey, or Helen Frankenthaler. Art that isn't a picture or representation of objects, but a display of form, texture, and color in and of themselves.

- Now look at the world. Look at sidewalks, walls, dirt, building sites. Perhaps focus in on small areas where there are patterns in the raw material.

- Can you see the world as abstract patterns of form, texture, and color?

- What if the world had no meaning other than form, texture, and color?

Again, don't bother with analyzing the art or the world. Don't bother with believing that any of this is true. Don't bother with judging your experience. Just play with what happens when you look at the world as if it were abstract art.

If you really don't like abstract art, try this with regular (figurative) art:

- Look at a painting of a figure or a still life or a landscape

- Notice that the entire canvas is made of paint, not just the figure.

- Notice your awareness is like that.

# *What Is This Happening In?*

*Game and variations*

- For each of the below, ask "What is this happening in?"
    - sound
    - images
    - sights
    - thoughts
    - emotions
    - body awareness
    - sense of self
    - time.

It can be fun to think of each of these as foreground with a corresponding background. Or content with a corresponding container.

For instance,

Sound happens in a field of silence.
Sights and images appear on the empty screen of vision.
Thoughts and emotions appear in the empty mind.
Your body image appears in space.
Your sense of self appears in the field of awareness.
Time appears in the endless Now.

*The next series of six games are specific examples of these:*

### The Sounds of Silence

- Play with each sound as it pops into awareness, and listen for the space of silence before and after each sound.

- Imagine that each sound appears in a field of silence.

- Slightly shift your focus from the sounds to the silence they appear in.

### The Movie Screen of My Mind

*Or "The Blank Canvas of My Mind" or "The Whiteboard of My Mind"*

- What do I see?

- Where does it appear?

- Can you imagine it appearing on a movie screen? (Or a blank canvas or a sheet of white paper or a whiteboard)?

- What if I'm the blank screen?

### The Empty Mind

- What if my mind were an empty vessel for thoughts and emotions to pop into?

- What if my mind was unaffected by thoughts and emotions? Thoughts come, thoughts go—the mind stays the same. Feelings come, feelings go—the mind is unaffected.

### Body in Spaciousness

- Where is the feeling of my body felt? Is it in my body? Maybe... play with it.

- What about the sense of my whole body? Where does that appear?

- Play with the feeling that the sense of body happens in a space that surrounds your body—that's a little bigger than, and outside of, your body.

### Big I and Little Me

- What if your sense of self is a little "me" that appears in a big "I"?

- What is the Big I that the Little Me appears in?

### Time and Now

- What is time? Who knows? But we can make a game of how we think about time. (It's about time.)

- What if "Now" is an empty vessel that time appears in?  What if "Now" is the eternal, infinite, everlasting, never-ending, vast field of the present that contains each single moment as it happens?

In other words, the background is what objects appear in, silence is what sound appears in, mind is what thoughts appear in, space is what the body appears in, "I" is what "me" appears in, and now is what time appears in.

Can you get a sense of this without thinking too much about it? Certainly don't give a moment's thought to whether all this is true or not. That's not what matters. What matters is your sense of it when you sort of "feel into it."

## *I Exist*

- Think the thought, "I exist."
- Notice what that feels like.
- How do you know you exist?
- See if you can answer that question without words or concepts, but only by noticing the feeling of existing, of being.

*Continuing in that vein...*

## *How Do I Know...?*

- How do I know I exist?
- What's the evidence?
- Outside of thought, what's the evidence?

## *Just Be*

*Or*
*You Can't See It, You Can Only Be It*

- Toss this around:
  An O'Connor koan:
  Is there anything I can think of that isn't seen by something I can't think of?
- What is that something?

You can't see it, you can only be it.

# *Body Games*

*A suite of games to play with your body awareness*

## *Big Body*

This game is an expansion of the mini-game, "Body in Spaciousness," above. And I do mean "expansion."

- Notice your body. Notice all of it. Keep noticing until you're noticing your entire body, from the top of your head to the tip of your toes, including every inch of skin, and every particle of every organ, and every physical sensation that appears.

- Now, imagine that you have a bigger body that surrounds and encompasses your entire body.

- Be that bigger body. Look at your regular body from that big body that surrounds it. Imagine that anything you can sense about your regular body is contained within Big Body.

- After you try out "Big Body" sitting down, try getting up and walking around a bit, all the while noticing your regular body from Big Body.

- Return to sitting or lying down, and let your Big Body expand. Let it be big enough to include everything you see, hear, and feel. If you hear sounds, imagine them happening inside your Big Body. If you look around the room, or out the window, imagine that everything you see is inside your Big Body.

## *Russian Doll*

*A variation on the Big Body game, based on the Russian* matryoshka *nesting dolls, only in reverse*

- Notice your body.
- Imagine a slightly bigger body noticing the smaller body.
- Imagine the bigger body containing the smaller body.
- Imagine a slightly bigger body noticing and containing that body.
- Imagine a slightly bigger body noticing and containing that body.
- Imagine that body in a bigger body.
- Be the bigger body.
- Imagine that body in a bigger body.
- Be the bigger body.
- Imagine that body in a bigger body.
- Be the bigger body.
- Imagine that body in a bigger body.
- Be the bigger body.
- Imagine that body in a bigger body.
- Be the bigger body.
- Et cetera, ad infinitum, world without end, аминь.

## *Where in the Body...?*

- Where in the body do I feel emotion?
- What does it feel like?
- What does it look like?

I used to think emotion was this amorphous non-physical thing that took over my mind. But I eventually realized that all emotions are actually chemical reactions in the body. When you have an emotion, especially one you don't like, it helps to look inside to discover where in the body that emotion is taking place.

Then, when you locate the area (or areas) in the body where the emotion appears, get curious. Just slow down, and watch.

There is a counterintuitive but profound truth about emotions, especially the so-called negative emotions: They just want to be noticed, not to be fixed, or analyzed. When they are given attention and allowed to be just the way they are, they shift.

It's as if they're saying, "Ah, finally, you're paying attention. Now feel me. Don't ignore me. Don't try to change me. Don't try to get rid of me. Just feel me. I have a message I need to deliver, and the more you relax and let me sing my singing telegram, the faster I'll sing it and move on. P.S. I love you."

## *Who Has a Body?*

- Think the thought "I have a body."
- Then ask yourself, "Who is this 'I' that has a body?"

## *Watch Yourself*

In your imagination...

- Stand in front of yourself and watch yourself.
- Hover above yourself and watch yourself.

## *Subject / Object Swap*

*Flipping back and forth in your mind between perceived objects and pure subjectivity.*

Here's how to get a taste for pure subjectivity:

- Look at an object. Any object—a cup for instance. Note that you are perceiving it. It's an object. You are the subject. So in this subject/object relationship, you're the subject and the cup is the object.

- Now look at your hand. Note that you are perceiving it. It's an object. You are the subject. So in this subject/object relationship, you're the subject and your hand is the object.

- Now think about an elephant. Note that you are having the thought. In this case, the thought of an elephant is an object. You are the subject. So in this subject/object relationship, you're the subject and the thought is the object.

- Now think about yourself. Note that you are having the thought. In this case, the thought of yourself is an object. You are the subject. So in this subject/object relationship, you're the subject and the thought of yourself is the object.

What's the difference between you and the thought about you? That difference is a pointer to pure subjectivity.

- When you get the feel for it, see if you can flip back and forth between awareness of an object and being the subject, and try it out on this list of subjects:
  - things
  - thoughts
  - feelings
  - images
  - ideas and concepts.

## *Content / Context Toggle*

This game is practically identical to "Subject / Object Swap," but some people might find it easier to think in terms of content and context.

- Notice something. Anything. Start with a simple object like a cup. Where is it? On a table? If so, the cup is the content, and the table is the context.

- Flip back and forth in your mind between the cup and its context, the table.

- Think about the cup. Notice your thought. Where is it? Where is the thought? In your mind? If so, the thought is the content, and your mind is the context.

- Flip back and forth between the thought and its context, your mind.

- Think about your mind. Notice your mind. Where is it? Is it in you? If so, your mind is the content, and you are the context.

- Flip back and forth between your mind and its context, you.

- Think about you. Notice your image of yourself. Where is it? Where is the image of yourself? Is it in pure context? If so, you are the content, and pure context is the context.

- Flip back and forth between you and pure context.


Also try "Foreground / Background Flip," which is the same game with different words.

# *Foreground / Background Flip*

This game is identical to "Content / Context Toggle," but you may find it easier. Or you may find "Content / Context Toggle" easier. Or you may find "Subject / Object Swap" easier. Whichever is more fun is the one to play.

- Notice something. Anything. Start with a simple object like a cup. Where is it? On a table? If so, the cup is the foreground, and the table is the background.

- Flip back and forth in your mind between the cup and its background, the table.

- Think about the cup. Notice your thought. Where is it? Where is the thought? In your mind? If so, the thought is the foreground, and your mind is the background.

- Flip back and forth between the thought and its background, your mind.

- Think about your mind. Notice your mind. Where is it? Is it in you? If so, your mind is the foreground, and you are the background.

- Flip back and forth between your mind and its background, you.

- Think about you. Notice your image of yourself. Where is it? Where is the image of yourself? Is it in pure background? If so, you are the foreground, and pure background is the background.

- Flip back and forth between you and pure background.

## *Be a Mirror*

- Imagine you're a mirror.

- Ask yourself: Am I choosing what to reflect?

- Or ask yourself: Am I practicing "reflection without selection"?

- Is the content real?

What if you stood in front of a mirror holding up two objects—a cup and a banana—one in each hand? What if the mirror decided, "I think I'll reflect the cup, but not the banana—I don't like fruit today."? Not too likely, eh?

Awareness is like that. At least pure unfiltered awareness is like that. It doesn't choose the content to be aware of. Your eyes see something—it's in awareness. Your ears hear something—it's in awareness. Be pure unfiltered awareness. It's already there; you don't have to find it.

Be that mirror.

## *Thought Picking*

*A very simple game—you win it if you lose it*

- Try to choose your thoughts.

Try to pick and choose your thoughts. Try to decide ahead of time what thoughts will appear and what thoughts will not.

If you fail, as I'm guessing you will (at least most of the time), then you will learn something fundamental. That is, if when you fail, you give up.

Here's a variation  The first one I played as a kid:

## *The Pencil Game*

- Imagine a pencil standing vertically on its point.
- Try to imagine it not falling down.
- If you succeed in imagining it not falling down, try to imagine it falling down and staying down without popping back up by itself.

If you're like me, at best you can only do one of these things, and sometimes neither. Try as you might, your mind has other ideas. This is similar to Daniel Wegner's example "don't think of a white bear." (He's the guy who wrote *White Bears and Other Unwanted Thoughts* and *The Illusion of Conscious Will*.)

## *Think About Anything You Want Except the Past and the Future*

Have you ever tried to stop your mind?  Have you ever tried one of those spiritual practices that ask you to stop thinking?  Well, here's a game that gives you permission to think... except there's a catch.

- Think anything you want to except for thoughts about the future or thoughts about the past.

- If thoughts about the future or thoughts about the past come up, let them go and see what else there is to think about that's not about the future or the past.

*Note: The above tiny little game is actually major.*

Here are two variations, one for future; one for past:

### *Future Fishing*

- Let your mind wander. Let it go where it will. And it will.

- Think of your mind as a stream that passes in front of you.

- Imagine you're fishing in that stream. But instead of fish, you're fishing for thoughts about the future.

- As soon as you catch a future thought, reel it in and pull it out of the thought stream. Maybe put it in a little box or basket behind you or beside you on the shore.

- See if you can clear your thought stream of thoughts about the future.

### *Past Catching*

- Let your mind wander. Let it go where it will. And it will.

- Imagine you're in a boat on a lake. Now imagine the lake is your mind.

- Imagine you're fishing off the side of that boat in the lake of your mind. But instead of trying to catch fish, you're trying to catch thoughts about the past.

- As soon as you catch a past thought, reel it in and put it in a little box or basket behind you or beside you in the boat.

- See if you can catch enough past thoughts so that the lake is clear.

When you get good at each of these, try doing them both together.

## *Doing Their Best*

*I love this one*

- What if everyone in the world were doing the best that they possibly can?

- Including you. What if you were doing the best that you possibly can?

Did I mention I love this one?

## *Find the Consciousness*

*A hide-and-seek game with your self*

- Look for your consciousness.

- Where is it?

- Don't define it, just find it.

- Don't settle for an idea about it. Don't settle for a concept of it. Only settle for the knowing of it for yourself.

A lot of great philosophers and neuroscientists are very active right now in an attempt to explain consciousness, and to find the source and cause of consciousness. I enjoy reading them (or at least reading about them), and following the debate over what is referred to as "the hard problem" (how and why we have experiences at all).

So let's help them out. But not by figuring it out for them—they're already hard at work on that—but by doing the leg-work, by looking for it first-hand inside our own minds. What a concept!  Instead of theorizing about it, going inside to look for it!  Then let us all know what you find.

## Particles, Waves, and Strings

*This is not really about physics*

- Imagine your body made up of tiny moving particles, or waves, or vibrating strings (whichever suits your fancy).

- Imagine the same about the air around you.

- Imagine the same about the objects around you.

- Imagine the same about the people around you.

- Imagine the same about the air that flows through you.

- Can you exist without the air?

- Are you separate from the air that flows through you?

- Are you separate from the other stuff that's also made of particles, or of waves, or of vibrating strings?

Try it first with particles, then with waves, then with vibrating strings, and then play with the one you like best.

## *Thinking in Tongues*

*Experiencing the words in your mind as a foreign language*

- Pick any language you don't understand.

- Imagine all the verbal thoughts inside your head are in that language.

- Don't try to understand them. Just luxuriate in the inner cluelessness about what your thoughts are trying to tell you.

- Since you can't understand any of your verbal thoughts, gradually shift your attention away from them, and towards whatever else is in your awareness.

This game is wonderful for dethroning your mental dialogue. Imagine someone coming up to you and talking non-stop in a foreign language you don't know, without realizing you're not understanding a single word. Eventually you just smile and nod, and let your mind wander elsewhere.

Only this time it doesn't wander to more words, but only to whatever nonverbal content appears in your awareness.

## *Experience Your Face from the Inside*

- Think of your face. Is the first image that pops up the picture of your face as it looks to you in the mirror?

- If so, try to imagine what it's like to experience your face from the inside.

Try it with your eyes closed and imagine feeling the inside of your face.

Try it with your eyes open and imagine seeing the inside of your face. When you're looking out through your eyes, notice what parts of the outside of your face you can actually see. (For me it's at most the tip of my nose or my upper lip if I scrunch it up.) Then imagine any parts that you can't see aren't really there.

## *The Finger Game*

- Run two fingers of the same hand along two different surfaces, such as your lap and the arm of your chair.

- Imagine how each finger is unaware of what the other feels, but you are aware of both.

- Now step back to an imaginary bigger picture. Imagine you're one finger and the person next to you is the other finger. Is there a bigger you who's aware of both your thoughts and the other person's thoughts?

Ok, I admit this one's a bit heady. It's really just a clumsy analogy for universal, non-local awareness, if there is such a thing. And there doesn't have to be such a thing for you to enjoy imagining there is. That's the thing about these games. They're not about what's true or not true. They're about what works. If this one works for you fine— play with it. If not, skip it. But don't skip the next one—it can come in really handy on a bad day. And don't expect to never have bad days again.

## *The Bad Mood Game*

*Playing with your mood*

When a bad mood strikes, play "The Bad Mood Game." "The Bad Mood Game" has five steps: Investigate it, play with it, investigate some more, then inquire, and finally, imagine. But don't worry about the exact steps in the exact order. They're there to inspire you to play it your way. It's your game.

Things to do with a bad mood:

1.  Investigate it:
    What if you didn't try to make it go away, but instead, got curious about it? Just for a few seconds, postpone doing anything to prevent feeling the way you feel, and investigate how you know that you feel what you feel.

    o   What are the signs of a bad mood? How do you know you're in a bad mood? What's the evidence? (Hint: It's usually in the body.) What does it feel like? What does it look like? Ask until you have an object inside with its own shape, color, feel, size, texture.

    o   Do you think you shouldn't be in a bad mood?

    o   Why shouldn't you be?

    o   Did you decide to be in a bad mood, or did it just show up?

    o   Is it inside you? Where? Where are its edges in relation to the edges of you?

    o   What if you could picture it in all its details?

2.  Play with it:
    What if you didn't try to make it go away, but instead, played with it—like food you didn't feel like eating?

    o   Can you make it grow? Can you make it larger?

- o Can you bring it down to where it was, and then back up again?
- o Can you make it louder?  And back?
- o Can you make it darker?  And back?
- o Can you make it rougher?  And back?
- o What parts of you do you feel it in?  Can you move it around from part to part?
- o Can you dial it up and down?  Don't try to dial it down all the way until it's gone—we want to play with it awhile. (Oops. Is it gone?  Oh well, next time.)

3. Investigate some more:

- o What does it eat?  What thoughts and stories does it trigger?  In other words, what thoughts does it feed on?  What thoughts make it grow?  What thoughts are the opposite—which ones would not be allowed if you wanted to keep the bad mood going?
- o What if you had no way of getting rid of a bad mood—if it was impossible to get rid of?  No hope.
- o What if you had no desire to get rid of it?  You wanted it to stay. "Please, don't go away—whatever you do, just stick around, please!"
- o What if you had absolutely no power over it?
- o What if you welcomed it in all its ugliness?

4. Inquire:

- o Who pictures it?
- o Who or what notices the bad mood?
- o What is it that's aware of all the sensations of a bad mood?

- o What parts of the bad mood don't need thought to be noticed?

- o What if the thoughts, stories, inner dialogues, past conversations, future dialogues—in other words, everything having to do with words—disappeared or went silent, or were in a foreign language? What parts of the bad mood would be left? Can you experience the bad mood without going to words?

5. Imagine:

- o What if the bad mood was there to protect you?

- o What if it was a big dumb guard sworn to never leave your side—ever since you were a baby—and protect you from all the mean, dangerous people or things that might hurt a little defenseless baby and make it cry? Could you thank the guard for years of loyal service?

- o Check back—who or what is aware of the guard?

Here's a possible dialogue you could have with yourself. Substitute bad, sad, or any other feeling for mad.

"I'm mad."
"How do you know?"
"What do you mean, how do I know?"
"How do you know you're mad?"
"I don't know, I just know."
"But how do you know?"
"I just feel mad."
"What's the evidence?"
"My jaw is clenched."
"Ah, now we're getting somewhere. What else?"
"My face feels hot"
"What else?"

"There's a knot in my stomach"

"Anything else"

"I'm having thoughts of doing severe bodily harm to the other person."

"Ha ha, great!"

"What do you mean, great?"

"I mean great—you succeeded in finding out how you know you're mad. Some of it was in your thoughts, and a lot of it was in your body."

"Yeah."

"How do you feel now?"

"Not so mad. (Or "I still feel mad." Either way is ok.)

"Cool."

That's a lot, I know. But a bad mood is worth the effort. But if the above is too much, here's a simple game:

## *Mood Children*

- Imagine that all your moods are children that you love equally. Doesn't the bad mood have just as much right to be here as the good mood? Welcome it with open, loving arms, don't banish it, spank it, or send it to bed without supper.

# *What is Effortless?*

A lot of spiritual-type teachings mention effortlessness. But in Awareness Games there is a tiny bit of effort. It's finding the least amount of effort possible to keep focused on awareness itself. Lots of effort and pure awareness eludes you. No effort and your mind just wanders into daydreams or into plans for the future, or into endless instant replays of past events. Too much effort and you find yourself trying to control your experience. How much effort is just enough to keep awareness gently on awareness itself instead of on the content of awareness, and no more?

### *Focus on Effortless Presence*

However, there are some phenomena that are effortless. You are present. You don't have to exert any effort to be present. You exist. You're here and that's the way it is. No effort required.

You are aware. Things appear in awareness effortlessly. Thoughts appear with no effort. Emotions and sensations appear with no effort (unless you want certain ones to appear at certain times, and then it's often no dice).

It can be fun to softly be aware of the things that happen effortlessly, and just let them happen effortlessly, while reserving that tiny least amount of effort necessary to be aware of awareness.

- Ask yourself, "What is effortless in my experience right now?"
    - Is hearing effortless?
    - Is seeing effortless?
    - Is feeling effortless?
    - Is thinking effortless?
    - Is awareness effortless?

## Further observations on Effortlessness

Effortlessness vs. Zero effort:

It takes zero effort to watch TV. It takes zero effort to sit and let your mind wander.

Effortlessness, on the other hand, requires a certain vigilance, which is the least amount of effort necessary to keep your attention on pure awareness (which is effortless) instead of on the content of awareness.

It's the least amount of effort needed to have no intention but to allow everything to be as it is. The least amount of effort needed to keep your focus off words but on the silence prior to words instead. The least amount of effort needed to keep your focus on direct experience rather than imagined experience of the past and future. Real reality instead of the virtual reality of thoughts. Being or thinking.

So effortlessness doesn't mean not trying. Effortlessness is not the relinquishing of personal action, but instead the recognition of the effortlessness that already exists in pure choiceless awareness. Pure being is effortless. But you have to try in order to recognize it.

## *What Is Thought?*

This is a great question to take the focus off the content of thought. The content of thought will never make you happy. It wants to lead you in the opposite direction, because its goal is to figure out what needs to change and how to change it.

But asking what thought *is* puts you outside of thought. That's where the real goodies are.

- What is thought?

- Where does it come from?

- What does it appear to?

- What's it made of?

- Does it happen by itself?

Remember, these are not questions to be answered with facts. That's for the neuroscientists (and I'm a big fan of neuroscientists). But these questions are designed to turn the focus of your mind around—from concepts to the space that concepts appear in. To be outside of thought, you can't just create thought about thought— that's just more thought. Instead you have to *feel* your way outside of thought, and be the thing that thought appears in. (Or better yet, the nothing that thought appears in.)

A fun variant of this is the next game...

## *Noticing and Experiencing*

If being aware of awareness doesn't work for you, play around with "noticing," or with "experiencing."

In other words, ask yourself "what am I noticing?" and "Who or what is doing the noticing?"

Or ask yourself "what am I experiencing?" and "Who or what is doing the experiencing?"

### *Who's Noticing That?*

- Try asking this whenever and wherever you remember to:
  Who's noticing that?    and who's noticing that?   ...and who's noticing that?

### *Noticing Without Words*

- What can I notice without words?

Or this variant:

- What can I notice without labeling?

### *Who Is Experiencing This?*

*(Or "Who is aware of this?")  (Or "Who is noticing this?")*

- Who or what is experiencing...
  - sound
  - sights
  - images
  - bodily sensations
  - emotions
  - thoughts
  - body awareness
  - sense of self?

## *Watch the Retrievers*

*I'd call it "Dog Zen" but that's already taken.*
*(See "Recommended Reading and Viewing.")*

Once when I was visiting some friends who had a house in the country, I spent a lot of time playing with their dog, Buddy, a golden retriever. Buddy had taken his retriever nature to obsessive extremes. He had a stone from the garden, a smooth stone, just the right size for him to carry in his mouth. He would find a likely human suspect and drop the stone at his or her feet. Since I was new and not yet sick of this game I was elected on that day. I picked up the stone and tossed it into the nearby woods. Buddy ran in, found it, ran back and dropped it my feet again. Again I'd pick it up and throw it. Again Buddy would retrieve it and drop it at my feet. If I walked away, Buddy would pick it up and follow me, dropping it at my feet in my new spot. If I didn't pick it up and throw it again, Buddy would bother me, poking my leg with his nose, or making whimpering noises or sometimes even barking. He never got tired of retrieving that stone no matter how many times I threw it. It didn't seem like he had any choice. He was a retriever. Retrieving was his nature, so that's what he did—retrieve.

Years later, I noticed that I had several recurring thought patterns that were like Buddy—compulsively going after some goal over and over no matter what. One of them was "How am I going to fix my life?" and its variants, "How can I make more money?" "How can I improve my career?"

Another retriever thought pattern was "I don't like this feeling. How can I make it go away and make sure it never happens again?" And another, "I did something wrong. How can I make sure no one notices, or make it seem like it was not my fault?"  Or "How can I avoid criticism and get only praise?"

These retriever thoughts are automatic. I don't decide to have them. If I could, I'd decide never to have them. But a retriever thought just keeps happening, never tiring; always ready to poke me with its nose to get my attention.

So the game is:

- Watch the retriever thoughts.
- Notice that they happen automatically.
- Notice that they aren't you.
- Identify with the bigger self that notices the retrievers.
- Don't try to stop them—let 'em retrieve. Just notice them, and notice they aren't you. You are much, much bigger and much more spacious.

Of course, one thing I haven't mentioned. You don't have to keep picking up the rock and throwing it. Buddy will nudge and whine and cajole for a while, but he'll eventually give up.

## *Slippery Mind*

- Imagine your mind is a very slippery, very smooth surface with no walls or fences or anything to hold on to.

- When a thought comes in, it can't stay—it's too slippery. It just—whoosh—slides on out the other side.

- Sometimes a thought will circle for a while before it slides out. When you notice this happening, just slightly tilt the smooth surface, and the thought will slip and slide right on out the other side.

Don't try to control the thoughts that come. Just let whatever thought that wants to come in come in. Then let it slide out again and wait for the next one to come.

The image I use for this is of a spinning disk in an old-fashioned funhouse. The one from my childhood at Playland in Rye, NY was shaped like a giant vinyl record, and had a highly polished smooth wooden floor. Kids would sit on it when it wasn't moving and then try to stay on it when it started spinning. Eventually we would slide off it from the centrifugal force. Some people said it had little random electric shocks, so people who were able to stay on the disk due to the friction of their clothing would shift their weight in reaction to the shock and slide right off the disk.

- So if some thoughts stick around in your slippery mind and continue to spin, you can nudge them with a little jolt and watch them slide right out.

## *Solid Block of Awareness*

*Awareness is one thing*

When you ask yourself, "What am I aware of?" the usual response may be something like, "the sounds outside, the way my body feels, the temperature of the room, my thoughts," etc.

- What if, instead of thinking of awareness as a catalogue of disparate items, you thought of it as one solid thing? One single block of awareness, or one solid sheet of awareness?

- Really try to include everything appearing in your awareness in this moment.

- If it helps, imagine it's all in a single picture frame, or in a single TV or movie screen, or in a single 3-dimensional sphere.

*Here's a fun variation...*

## *The Blender*

*A recipe for one taste*

Notice everything that's in awareness and blend it all into one delicious smoothie.

- Pour all your sights in to a blender.

- Add all your sounds.

- Scoop in all your bodily sensations.

- Sprinkle in everything you smell and taste.

- Ladle in all your feelings and emotions.

- Drizzle in all your thoughts.

- Blend.

- Enjoy.

## *Real Reality vs. Virtual Reality*

*In praise of Direct Experience*

What is direct experience? It is everything that is perceived in the current moment thorough the senses, and nothing that is remembered, imagined, conceptualized, or verbalized.

It is real reality as opposed to virtual reality.

Virtual reality includes daydreaming, fantasizing, mulling over, and most automatic thinking.

So here's the game...

- Notice direct experience.
- Notice everything about it.
- Notice it without labeling any of it with words.
- Notice the experiencing.
- Look for an experiencer.

Some flags to help you notice you're in virtual reality instead of direct experience:

You're remembering a past event.

You're imagining the future.

You're thinking about the last thought you had.

You're ignoring your senses.

You're trying to change your experience.


Fully experiencing present reality requires an open-minded curiosity and an open-hearted intimacy with all experience, so leave your opinions and conclusions at the door while playing this game.

## *Catch the Next Trance*

*Directly related to the previous game*

Virtual reality (the way I've defined it) is a kind of a trance. In order to wake yourself up from a trance you need to be able to recognize when you're in a trance and when you're not.

Here's how:

- Notice any of these clues that you're in a trance:
    - you're lost in thought
    - you're imagining a future event
    - you're reliving a past event
    - you're thinking about fixing or changing anything.
- You're not in a trance when:
    - you're noticing any of the above
    - you're aware of everything that's in awareness right now
    - you're aware of awareness itself.

## *Four Ultra-Simple Games*

### *Try Not To*

- Just for a few minutes...
    - Try not to want anything.
    - Try not to get anything.
    - Try not to achieve anything.
    - Try not to plan anything.
    - Try not to do anything.
    - Try not to think of anything.

Try this just for now—Just for a short while. You can always go back to wanting, getting, achieving, planning, doing, and thinking later. If you want to.

### *The Yes Game*

- Say yes to everything in your mind.
- Even to your mind saying no.

It doesn't matter what the content is. Just let whatever comes come, and say "Yes."

### *Just non-do it*

- Catch yourself doing something.
- Then do nothing.

But isn't playing a game doing something? Paradox alert! You non-figure it out.

### *No Thoughts*

- Imagine what it would be like to not have any thoughts.

## Two-Person Game

*Here's one you can play with someone else. Take turns.*

- Player A asks Player B, "What are you?"
- Player B responds.
- Whatever Player B says, Player A replies, "That's not what you are."

Some possible Player B responses: "I'm a woman," "I'm a man," "I'm <your name here>," "I'm this body," "I'm the other person in the room," "I'm my thoughts," "I am what I feel." All these are "wrong" answers in this game.

Some other possible Player A replies: "Nope," "That's not you," "Sorry," "Try again." If A is sensitive, B should be nice. If A and B are trusting and close, it can be ruder. Like a buzzer or a Bronx cheer.

Player B should not try to get it right, or to avoid "wrong" answers, but simply report what he or she seems to be at that moment.

## Free the World

*You want freedom for yourself?  Set the rest of the world free first.*

- Set the world free from your judgments of it.
- Set the world free from your opinion of it.
- Set the world free from your expectations of it.

Is this really a game?  Maybe not. Maybe it's a time-out, during which you will do no refereeing.

Here are some other time-out games...

## Judgment Day

It might be better to call this "Notice Judgment Day."  The idea isn't to judge or not judge, but just to be aware of your judgment.

- For one day, notice every time you judge something, someone, or yourself.
- No need to do anything about it. Meaning no need to express your judgment; no need to stop judging; no need to get down on yourself for judging.
- Just say to yourself, "I'm judging," or "I'm aware I'm judging," or "There I go again, judging. Funny, eh?"

## *Non-Judgment Day*

*For advanced players.*

- For one day, don't judge anything or anybody, including yourself.
- If that's too hard, try half a day, or one hour, or one minute.

And remember, this isn't "Condone Evil Day," or "Let People Get Away with Hurting Other People Day." You don't even need to believe that people who break the rules shouldn't be punished. It simply means, for one day, try not to judge them if they do.

This goes for the next game too...

## *Forgive*

- Forgive everybody for everything. No matter what. Including yourself.
- Forgive yourself for everything you just did, you're doing now, or thinking about doing.

You may find yourself thinking, "Whoa... people shouldn't forgive themselves for everything. We'd be overrun with sociopaths who would do whatever it pleased them to do!" If so, remember this: It's impossible for anyone who has forgiven everyone, including themselves, for everything, to be a sociopath—or even a garden-variety mean, nasty person. On the contrary, if you forgive everyone, including yourself, of everything, you can't help but love unconditionally. In fact, you will be love itself.

## *Schwooming*

*Schwoom the moment, schwoom the situation, schwoom the thought pattern*

*Schwooming* is kind of like doing all the Awareness Games at the same time.

I call schwooming schwooming because there is no word that includes all the inner things you can do to turn a rough moment into a joyful moment. It's a complex activity because it involves doing several things at once. But if you practice them individually, each one becomes second nature, so you really can do them all at the same time, and instantly.

The elements of schwooming:

1. Relax.
   Let go of any internal clutching, tension, tightening, or resistance.

2. Let it be.
   Allow everything to be as it is. Let go of looking for ways to change things—meaning anything: the situation, other people, yourself, your thoughts and feelings, their thoughts and feelings and opinions, the world around you.

3. Be awareness.
   Step back and be the background. Identify with pure awareness.

An example of schwooming:

Someone is in your way or has cut in front of you and you're annoyed. (This can be while driving, in a supermarket, on a subway or bus, at a sporting event, etc.) You start thinking about how that person shouldn't have done that. Maybe you even tell him or her off. Maybe you even feel bad about how you feel or how you reacted. Schwoom the moment.

To yourself, say "schwoom," because you know that means: relax physically and let go of inner tension, accept the moment exactly as it is, and notice the awareness that's noticing it all happening.

Try each element separately for a while until you can do it without much thought. Then start adding an element, until each schwoom encompasses all the elements of schwooming.

If you don't like the word *schwoom,* make up your own. Or try *Ahh...* or *Mmm...* or *blingalingaling,* or something like that. Whatever you like that comes to mean relaxing, allowing, aware-ing. (You can even call it *RAA.*)

You can schwoom a moment that just happened, schwoom a situation you find yourself in, schwoom a thought or memory that comes up, schwoom a judgment that arises—of others or of yourself, schwoom a person, schwoom a news story, schwoom an emotion.

And you don't have to only schwoom bad things. Why not schwoom the good things too?  All you have to do is substitute appreciating for allowing and *voila*—you're schwooming the good stuff too.

If you do all three schwooming elements fully in any given moment, you'll turn it into a moment of joy and peace. And if you master schwooming, and schwoom as often as possible, the schwoomed moments will coalesce into one big schwoomfest of a life.

## The Ultimate Game

*Be*

Did you notice that all the games are really variations of this game?

1. Be ok with whatever is happening now.

2. Be awareness.

In other words:

A) Relax and stop controlling.

B) Shift attention...
   *from...*
   how the outside world should change in order to get what you want...
   *to...*
   whatever it is inside you that never changes, that has never changed; that experiences the outside world, and always has.

Because when you change your focus to that inner witness, you relax and allow yourself to vibrate sympathetically with the world, and therefore flow more easily.

So...

- Be the Background.

- Just Be.

- Be.

- That's basically it.

B.

# *Tips and Traps*

## The Mind

Oh boy, does the mind ever want to take over and think, think, think! Fine. That's what it does. Who can blame it? When playing Awareness Games, as in meditation, the mind likes to hijack awareness and narrow it down. This is natural. It will happen. It happens to everybody. It will keep happening. Let it. Each time it does, and you *notice* that it does, you've won a little mini-awareness game. Just gently include the thoughts among all the other contents of awareness and step back into pure awareness itself.

## Easy First, Difficult Later

When you start to get the hang of it, and you notice that you get that lovely, happy-for-no-reason feeling while you're playing Awareness Games, you're bound to notice that when you stop playing, the feeling may or may not stick around. Especially when life's challenges call you to focus on solving a particular problem, or trigger a fear or anxiety or other unwanted emotion. This is natural.

Being awareness is a skill that you first apply to easy situations, and then gradually try out on more difficult ones. The idea is eventually to remain identified with pure awareness all the time. But don't kick yourself if this doesn't happen right away. Just keep playing, and eventually it will be there more and more of the time and during more and more challenging situations.

## Repetition

Oy yoy yoy, there's so much repetition in these Awareness Games! Yep. There's really only one Awareness Game. All the others are just attempts to get at the same thing from different angles. One angle may strike one person in just the right spot, but might leave another person cold. Besides, you have to tap away at the rock many times before it cracks.

## Awareness Reminders

The main thing is to remember to play Awareness Games as often as you can. So you can set reminders for yourself. For instance, if you like to play the "Feeling Music on the Inside" game, you can set a mental reminder that whenever you hear a particular song, or a particular piece of music, or type of music, or any music, you'll play that game or any of the games, even if it's only for a few moments.

You can actually make almost anything an awareness reminder. Like walking into a bookstore. Or seeing a shirt or blouse of a certain color. Or picking up your mail. Or hearing a bird, or a car horn. Or drinking a glass of water. If you set up enough reminders, eventually you'll be reminding yourself all day long, and you'll enjoy being awareness all day long, every day.

## Sidestep Logic

Don't fight with logic. I love logic. I'm good at logic. Logic is very useful for many things. But logic is not too helpful in Awareness Games. That's because we're trying to get the feel of what's behind thought, and logical conceptual thought can obscure it. Like a crowded museum on a Sunday and you want to look at Monet's water lilies, but there are just too many people in the way.

So if logic is activated, just say, "of course, that's right, thanks," and focus back on who's noticing it.

For instance, I often think things like, "You say we're all one, but I'm looking out through my eyes, I'm not looking out through your eyes, or Fred's eyes. That proves I'm separate from you or Fred." When you start to think things like that, say to yourself, "yes, of course, that's right, thanks." Then ask, "Who or what is having this thought? What's aware of this thought? What is awareness anyway? What's doing the 'aware-ing'?"

## Traps

The number one trap: Effort. It's not an advanced state you get to by working harder or being more disciplined or concentrating more. In fact, working harder may just be the obstacle in your way to noticing awareness and simply sitting back and being pure awareness itself.

The number two trap: Fixing things. If you are focused on changing or fixing the content of awareness, it's pretty darn near impossible to notice pure awareness itself. So at least while you're playing Awareness Games, just notice what's in awareness; don't try to fix or change what's in awareness.

The number three trap: Thinking too much. That includes analyzing, conceptualizing, philosophizing, and planning how you are going to describe your experience in words later when you are no longer experiencing it.

The number four trap: Seriousness. It's easier if you don't take anything too seriously. At least while you're playing Awareness Games.

The number five trap: Trying to get rid of what you're feeling right now. It's counterintuitive, but when I play an Awareness Game in order to get rid of an unwanted emotion, or even to create that feeling of happiness, it doesn't work. Simply play with noticing awareness itself and the happiness reveals itself, regardless of, and unrelated to whatever you may be feeling. (This could easily be the number one trap.)

# *Some Further Reflections*

### Enlightenment

I mentioned at the beginning that I don't consider myself an enlightened person. I define an enlightened person as someone who has seen through the illusion of being a separate person. I still feel like a separate person. Although it seems that the pure awareness in me is identical to the pure awareness in everyone else. And when I think that it might just be the same, universal, awareness, I'm filled with awe and joy.

I still have bad days, grumpy days, neurotic days. Actually these moods hardly last a whole day anymore. Call them bad hours, or grumpy spells. But now and then they do last the whole day—or longer. Still, every time I play an awareness game when some so-called negative emotion pops up, sooner or later I feel better, and in some mysterious way, things seem to work out better too. Not necessarily right away, but eventually.

If these grumpy days or sad spells or angry episodes happen to you, love yourself for being human, and play your favorite Awareness Game. If that one isn't working for you at the moment, try another. Of course they work better if you're just playing it for playing's sake, and not trying to actually change the grumpy mood.

The feeling of Awareness Games gradually starts to permeate your whole way of looking at and experiencing life. So why wait for enlightenment? Play now. Play often.

And if the illusion of separation falls away for me, I'll update this book (if there's another edition). If not, I'll continue to play with enjoying myself and life as much as possible, and I hope you will too.

And maybe, just maybe, the me that thinks awareness is *in* my mind, is actually *in* universal awareness, along with my mind and everyone else's.

## Philosophy

I'm not offering philosophy here; just stuff to do—stuff you can try, and see if it has an effect. Philosophy is great, and crucial to humanity, but it's not relevant to Awareness Games. Remember, philosophy is the menu, not the food. Sometimes it's more like a recipe, and sometimes it's more like a restaurant review in a newspaper. None of it can substitute for actual eating.

The same goes for metaphysics.

## Consciousness vs. Awareness

Some teachers and writers make a distinction between consciousness and awareness. Perhaps they have a point. Maybe consciousness is global and awareness is local. I suppose awareness can be directed or focused on different things and consciousness includes it all, although I usually think of this as pure awareness and local awareness. Most of the time, though, I have a hard time seeing the difference between consciousness and awareness, and I usually experience the two terms as interchangeable. So feel free to think of these as Consciousness Games if you prefer, or substitute the word "consciousness" for "awareness."

Some may define consciousness as that which disappears in deep sleep or under anesthesia. Fine. In that case, we can call that consciousness and awareness is what consciousness disappears *from,* and is waiting there for it to return.

## Self-Improvement

Instead of self-improvement, try self-enjoyment.

# *Acknowledgments*

The idea for *Awareness Games* grew out of theater games, pioneered by Viola Spolin, and taught to me (and to many, many others) by my mom, Lenka Peterson O'Connor. Thanks Mom!

For reading early drafts, attending trial game sessions, and for their advice, encouragement, love, and friendship, my heartfelt thanks go to Gautam Belday, Christina Dacauaziliqua, Ray Gaspard, Tanya Goff, Mina Hai, Darren O'Connor, Glynnis O'Connor Stern, Debra Vogel, Elfin Vogel, and especially Dana Cheng who has been a long-standing Awareness Games enthusiast.

Special thanks to Lindsay Stern for reading multiple drafts and for offering enormously helpful feedback, encouragement, and great discussions.

Special thanks also go to Bridgit Dengel Gaspard, whose inspiration, wisdom, game play-testing, and practical and emotional support, contributed immeasurably to this book.

Extra special thanks to my husband, Josh Yu for his love, support, and all around soul-mateship.

For their wisdom and teaching, thanks to these teachers, with whom I've met and studied: Stuart Schwartz and Loch Kelly. And to these teachers, whom I've never met and who have no idea who I am, but nonetheless have influenced me deeply: Adyashanti and Rupert Spira.

Thanking and acknowledging these teachers in no way constitutes their endorsement, permission, imprimatur, transmission, lineage, or any claims to be an official purveyor of their teachings. All errors in teaching, philosophy, and presentation are purely my own.

When I grow up, I want to be like these guys. Until then, I offer my own playful take on being awareness itself.

# Recommended Reading and Viewing

**Loch Kelly**
*Shift into Freedom: The Science and Practice of Open-Hearted Awareness* (Sounds True, 2015)
http://lochkelly.org/

**Stuart Schwartz**
http://www.satsangwithstuart.com/

**Dogzen**
http://www.sandoth.com/Dogzen.htm

**Adyashanti**
*Emptiness Dancing* (Sounds True, 2006)
*True Meditation* (Sounds True, 2006)
http://www.adyashanti.org/

**Rupert Spira**
http://rupertspira.com/

**Enza Vita**
*Always Already Free: Recognizing the natural wakefulness we were born with* (Baraka Publishing, 2015)
http://enzavita.com/

**Bridgit Dengel Gaspard**
http://www.bridgit-dengel-gaspard.com/

49994997R00055

Made in the USA
Lexington, KY
28 February 2016